The Fight for Survival

Andres Llamas Ruiz

Illustrations by Luis Rizo

Sterling Publishing Co., Inc.
New York

Illustrations by Luis Rizo
Text by Andrés Llamas Ruiz
Translated by Natalia Tizón

Library of Congress Cataloging-in-Publication Data

Llamas Ruiz, Andrés.
　　[Lucha por la supervivencia. English]
　　The fight for survival / by Andres Llamas Ruiz ; illustrations by
Luis Rizo.
　　　　p.　　cm. — (Cycles of life)
　　Includes index.
　　Summary: Examines the different forms of survival techniques of
mammals, insects, reptiles, and fish, describing how they capture
food and escape from predators.
　　ISBN 0-8069-9743-5
　　1. Competition (Biology)—Juvenile literature.　[1. Animals—
Habits and behavior.]　I. Rizo, Luis, ill.　II. Title.　III. Series:
Llamas Ruiz, Andrés.　Secuencias de la naturaleza.　English.
QH546.3.L5813　1997
591.5´3—dc21
　　　　　　　　　　　　　　　　　　　　　　　　　　　96–37954
　　　　　　　　　　　　　　　　　　　　　　　　　　　CIP
　　　　　　　　　　　　　　　　　　　　　　　　　　　AC

1　3　5　7　9　10　8　6　4　2

Published by Sterling Publishing Company, Inc.
387 Park Avenue South, New York, N.Y. 10016
Originally published in Spain by Ediciones Estes
©1996 by Ediciones Lema, S.L.
English version and translation © 1997 by Sterling Publishing Company, Inc.
Distributed in Canada by Sterling Publishing
℅ Canadian Manda Group, One Atlantic Avenue, Suite 105
Toronto, Ontario, Canada M6K 3E7
Distributed in Great Britain and Europe by Cassell PLC
Wellington House, 125 Strand, London WC2R 0BB, England
Distributed in Australia by Capricorn Link (Australia) Pty Ltd.
P.O. Box 6651, Baulkham Hills, Business Centre, NSW 2153, Australia
Printed and Bound in Spain

Sterling　ISBN 0-8069-9743-5

Table of Contents

The first moments of life are difficult

Did you know that there are more than five million different species of plants and animals?

All of them struggle their entire lives in order to survive, reach adulthood, and reproduce. However, birth and childhood are highly dangerous stages of the life-cycle—a period when the young are at the mercy of predators. This is why parents look after their offspring by feeding and protecting them until they can live on their own. In mammals, parental protection can last for years!

Animals have developed two different kinds of strategies to overcome the uncertainties of reproduction. Some parents lay many eggs or bear many offspring and then completely abandon them. Others have very few offspring, but they protect and look after the offspring until they can survive on their own.

2

3

Marsupials have developed a perfectly designed device to transport their offspring. Here you can see a female kangaroo carrying her baby in her pouch.

When relocating to their burrows or in the presence of danger, the parents of some carnivores transport their offspring by holding them delicately between their sharp teeth.

Animals of many species look after their babies to ensure that they will survive the first stages of life. During their "childhood," babies are fed, cleaned, transported, protected, etc.

1. From the moment they are born, baby mammals are fed with milk produced by their mothers.

2. Most amphibians lay their eggs in the water and then abandon them. However, some frogs take care of their babies by transporting them on their back.

3. For the first days, female scorpions transport their babies on their back in order to protect them with their stingers.

4. Little birds remain in their nest, waiting for their parents to return and feed them.

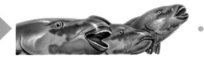

Some animals prefer to spend most of their lives alone or in couples

Jackals form stable couples to help raise their offspring.

Have you ever noticed that there are never too many predatory animals of the same species banding together?

Not all animals live in groups. There are many animals that spend their entire lives "alone" in their own territory, defending it from the attacks of other animals of the same species. This is particularly common in carnivores, which hunt alone because they cannot tolerate the presence of competitors in their territory. Adult females and males of these species usually remain isolated, except during brief reproductive periods. After they have mated, they separate and never see each other again. The female usually takes care of the offspring by herself, although sometimes it is the male who looks after the little ones without help from the female.

There are, however, other animals that mate for life. In these cases, the babies remain close to their parents to form a family group until the young have developed completely.

2

3

Some animals change their behavior as they grow. Barracudas, for example, travel in large schools while they are young, but the oldest and largest ones prefer to live alone.

Most felines (such as this puma) spend their lives as solitary animals, only meeting the opposite sex to reproduce.

Some animals are so solitary that they do not allow any other member of their species to enter their territory, except during the reproductive stage.

1. Many predatory animals, such as this lynx, spend most of their lives without contact with other members of their species.

2. Most snakes also live alone . . .

3 . . . although in some species all of them gather to spend the winter underground together.

4. In most bird species, both members of the couple take equal care of the babies because incubation and the search for food are very difficult tasks.

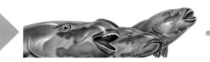

Sometimes animals form groups for protection

When animals of one species gather to live together, there are many possible combinations. For example, among mammals it is very common to have a harem in which a dominant male lives surrounded by several females of reproductive age. The number of females varies, depending on the species. The remaining younger males form groups and wait for the time when each will be old enough to form his own harem.

As the number of animals forming the group increases, the relationship among them becomes complicated and they form a complex hierarchy in which a group of dominant males retains power. This system has the advantage of being a good defense strategy against predators. When the group presents a united front, it can often defeat a predator too strong for any one of the males to beat alone. The males can also band together to help one another defeat rival males when they try to steal the group's females!

As part of a herd, musk oxen protect themselves from wolf attacks by forming a circle. If the herd has offspring, they are kept well within the defensive circle.

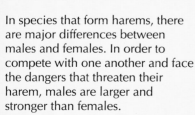

In species that form harems, there are major differences between males and females. In order to compete with one another and face the dangers that threaten their harem, males are larger and stronger than females.

1. When controlling his harem, the male makes sure that all offspring are his own.

2. Young males that do not have their own harem stay far away to form an isolated group.

3. When the head of a harem gets sick or grows old, a stronger male replaces him and takes over the harem.

4. After the reproductive stage, some groups separate. Deer, for example, divide into groups of males and females that do not meet again until the following year.

1

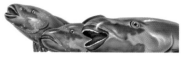

Elephants live in groups that are divided by sex. Babies of both sexes remain in herds made up of females.

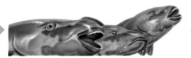

Some groups can be very large

Some groups are made up of hundreds or thousands of animals that stay together to migrate. In these gigantic nomadic groups, the animals meet and travel great distances. Some famous migrations are undertaken by herbivores (such as zebras and gnus), birds (whose enormous flocks travel through the skies), and salmon (which swim upstream to reproduce). Migratory animals can travel thousands of miles together!

Social insects have developed even more complex hierarchies. Their organizations are based on different types of members that share the work of the group in a very efficient way. Ants, termites, and many bees, as well as wasps, have caste systems with queens, drones, workers, and soldiers so that each does a very specific job! The members form a society in which the creatures put their common interests before their own, even sacrificing their lives for the colony.

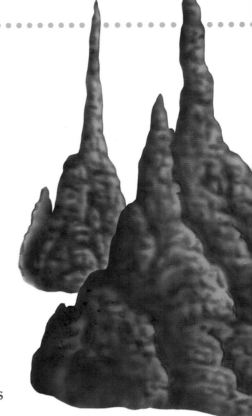

In species where many animals live together, it is necessary to perfect a communication system and achieve an efficient distribution of work. Social insects, such as bees and ants, represent the most extreme cases, since the animals are divided into castes with different appearances and jobs.

1. The queen ant lays eggs throughout her entire life.

2. Worker ants are in charge of searching for food, cleaning, feeding the babies and queen, etc.

3. Soldiers or sentinels defend the colony from enemy attack. The soldiers' jaws have adapted for this function to the degree that, in many cases, they would not be able to eat if they were not fed by the workers!

Termite nests are huge structures—up to 20 feet tall. More than five million termites may live inside.

Weaver birds build common living quarters that are formed by as many as one hundred individual nests. They are like apartment buildings!

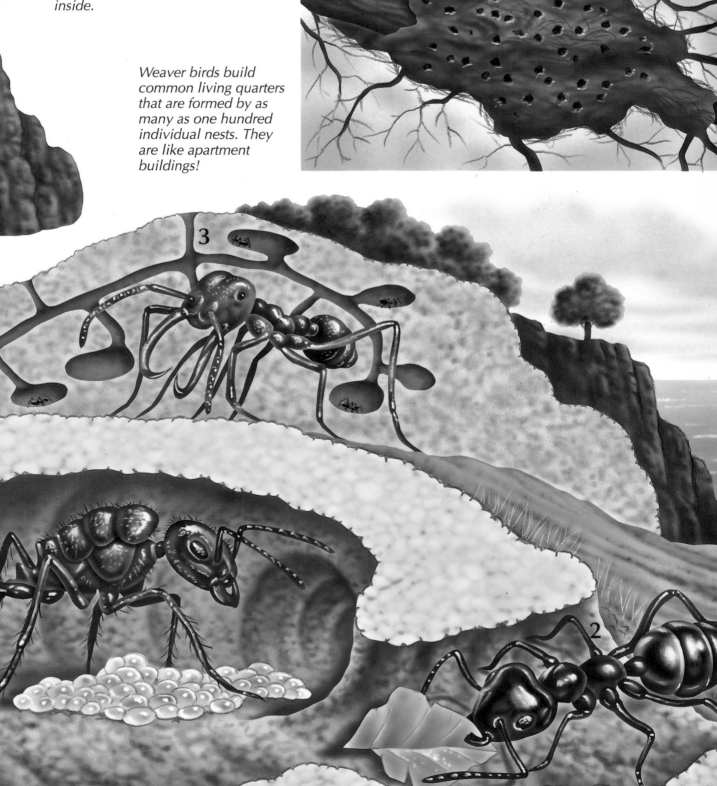

Sometimes animals face great changes

In order to survive, animals must not only protect themselves from their enemies but they must also deal with changes in their environment. Temperature, rain, and other weather conditions vary throughout the year. These climate changes force many species to adapt their behavior in order to reproduce during seasons when the weather is mild. During spring and summer, they also collect the food they will need to face the hard winter.

Living creatures are spread out across the world and occupy all types of places: oceans, deserts, mountains—even polar areas. The species have all evolved to survive in different conditions; only those who have adapted best to their environment have thrived!

1b

2

In coastal areas, tidal conditions change twice daily, making life difficult for creatures that make the shore their home.

1. Limpets (**a**) cling to the rocks; barnacles (**b**) close their powerful shells at low tide to avoid dehydration when they are exposed to the sun.

2. Mussels resist the waves by holding on to the rocks with their filaments, called byssal threads.

3. Sea urchins protect themselves from their enemies by covering their entire body with long, sharp quills.

4. Some birds live close to the sea, like these cormorants, in order to obtain their food by diving underwater.

Animals living in the desert must endure great temperature changes. Daytime temperatures are very high (up to 140°F), but nighttime temperatures can drop as low as freezing—32°F.

In mountainous areas, the arrival of the winter snow forces animals to adapt. Some, like this ptarmigan, change color in order to remain unnoticed during each season of the year.

WINTER

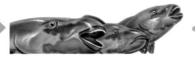
Individuals from different species can help each other overcome obstacles

Did you know that some animals of different species become "partners"?

Organisms of different species sometimes fight each other to the death. On the other hand, they sometimes collaborate in symbiotic relationships, which means they form partnerships to help each other survive.

For example, small animals sometimes clean and eliminate parasites that bother bigger animals. In these cases, the larger animal does not attack the small one, which could be very easy prey. During cleaning sessions, the smaller animals may even venture into the mouths of their larger "clients," to clean their teeth and tongue. The benefit of this kind of relationship is that the smaller animals obtain food and the larger ones are stripped of parasites. A great deal for both!

In the sea, the job of cleaning fish is extremely important. Without the help of smaller fish, the bigger ones would quickly die because of parasites and diseases.

The clownfish lives among the poisonous tentacles of the sea anemone. The little fish gains protection; in exchange, it helps the anemone by bringing it food.

3

2

The hermit crab has a soft, vulnerable abdomen. To protect it, the crab uses an empty snail shell and then also places one or several anemones on top of its abdomen. In exchange, the anemones can travel without too much effort.

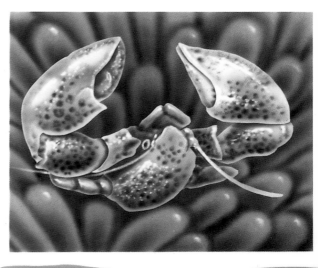

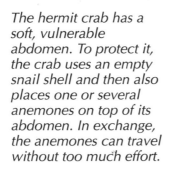

1

4

Undersea "cleaning stations" are common. Nearby fish go to these stations to rid themselves of parasites that stick to their bodies.

1. Cleaning shrimp remove parasites from the mouth of morays.
2. Cleaning blennies are experts in removing parasites from the gills of other fish.
3. Sometimes there are "lines" of fish waiting their turn to be cleaned up.
4. Remoras (shark suckers) attach themselves to sharks and move around their body to clean away parasites and dead skin.

As a defense, some species prefer to "disappear"

Animals always have to be alert and ready to escape immediate danger.

Most creatures spend their lives avoiding attacks by their predators. When they feel threatened, they often remain completely still. Why? The answer is that predators are on the alert, ready to detect the tiniest movement. It is often more difficult to spot a prey when it remains absolutely motionless.

Many "helpless" species have also developed intriguing methods of camouflage. This is especially true of those animals whose bodies are small, soft, and . . . delicious. They use different tricks to give themselves some advantages, such as adopting the color of their environment, covering their skin with irregular spots that camouflage their shapes, etc. The combination of alternating light and dark colors on an animal's body conceals its basic body form, although stripes and spots are sometimes specially placed to hide certain parts of the body, such as legs, eyes, neck, and wings.

Some butterflies, as well as other insects, achieve perfect camouflage, which makes them "invisible" to their predators. In this case, the wings imitate a dry leaf.

4

3

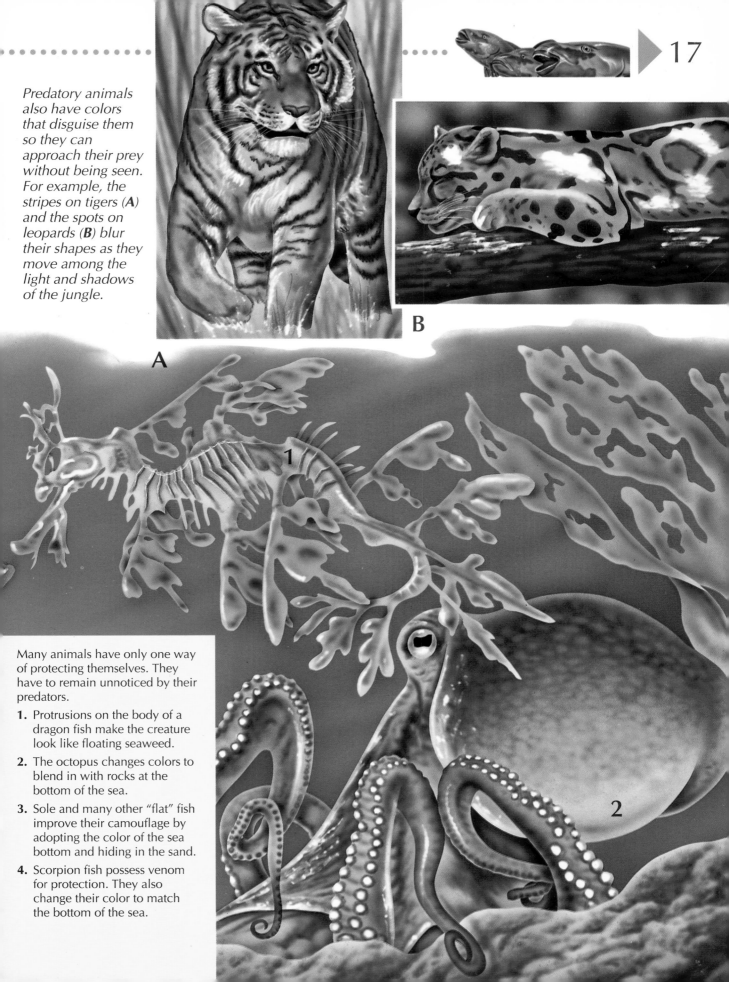

*Predatory animals also have colors that disguise them so they can approach their prey without being seen. For example, the stripes on tigers (**A**) and the spots on leopards (**B**) blur their shapes as they move among the light and shadows of the jungle.*

A

B

1

2

Many animals have only one way of protecting themselves. They have to remain unnoticed by their predators.

1. Protrusions on the body of a dragon fish make the creature look like floating seaweed.

2. The octopus changes colors to blend in with rocks at the bottom of the sea.

3. Sole and many other "flat" fish improve their camouflage by adopting the color of the sea bottom and hiding in the sand.

4. Scorpion fish possess venom for protection. They also change their color to match the bottom of the sea.

Others prefer to attract the attention of their parents

Have you ever noticed that some animals, instead of trying to camouflage themselves, are covered with very flashy colors? Why? These colors are aposematic, which means "warning signal." These signals prevent them from being attacked, since they show that the colorful animal has a very unpleasant taste—perhaps even poisonous glands. If a predator tries to eat one of these animals, it will have such a nasty experience it will never try again!

1

3

Bees and wasps warn potential enemies (especially birds) that they are not an easy meal. Do they dare to attack them?

Nudibranchs—or sea slugs—have a soft, unprotected body, so they accumulate toxic substances as protection from their enemies. To "warn off" their foes, these fish are covered with spectacular colors.

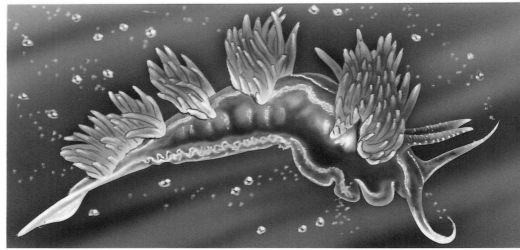

There is a wide range of animals (especially insects and amphibians) that use bright colors to warn their enemies. We can find aposematic combinations in butterflies, wasps, water snakes, etc.

1. Yellow and black markings may signify that an animal has an unpleasant taste or that, like this salamander, it possesses poisonous glands.

2. The smallest animals and those that seem the most vulnerable have spectacular color combinations.

3. The eastern fire-bellied toad has bright colors on its belly. When it senses danger, it turns "belly-up" and its warning becomes unmistakable.

4. These South American frogs, less than 2 inches long, are covered with one of the most powerfully known poisons to man. Their colors are unmistakable!

The best defense is always escape

Flying squirrels confuse their enemies by jumping from tree to tree, away from danger.

When a predator jumps toward its prey, there is only one option: to run full speed. Many species reach great speed during their escapes. Deer, for example, can run at 40 miles per hour and some antelopes speed along at more than 50 miles per hour.

However, many predators are faster than their prey. The fastest land animal is the cheetah. For a few seconds at a time, it can reach the speed of more than 75 miles per hour. The prey can escape, providing it maintains its own speed long enough. Once the chase starts, the results depend on the distance from which the hunter started and on the reaction and strength of the prey.

On the other hand, some predators, such as the wolf, prefer to tire out their prey by group hunting and chasing them for long distances.

Animals do not normally escape in a straight line. Many of them run in a zigzag pattern to confuse their predators. Other animals, such as frogs and grasshoppers, prefer to run and hide. If they are lucky, the predator will not find them.

When animals cannot hide from their predators and do not have any "weapons" to defend themselves, their last resort is to run.

1. When in danger, ostriches can reach great speeds.
2. Impalas escape with huge leaps and change directions to confuse predators.
3. Predators, such as this cheetah, know if their "prey" is sick or tired by the height of the jumps the prey makes as it escapes. Once a cheetah has spotted the weakest animal, it moves in for the kill.
4. There are animals, such as the oryx and the zebra, that do not follow a strategy in their escape. They just gallop away at full speed.

Slow animals, such as snails and turtles, are covered with sturdy shells to protect themselves from their enemies.

1

4

2

3

There are also animals that have other weapons for their defense

Not all animals run away from their enemies. Some have powerful weapons that allow them to confront their predators.

Armadillos and pangolins have protective shells that are formed by very hard plates. But the expert in armor is the turtle. A battery of sharp quills is another security system that turns animals, such as hedgehogs and porcupines, into a very bad-tasting meal. When these animals feel threatened, they curl their bodies into a ball (with the quills or the plates facing out), leaving no vulnerable point in their exterior.

Elephants and rhinoceroses have almost no enemies. They are almost invulnerable, thanks to their size and the sharpness of their tusks and horns. Their skin also provides remarkable protection; the skin of an adult elephant is more than an inch thick!

Skunks have a very effective chemical defense. They shoot a stream of stinking odor that is noxious when it reaches the delicate membranes of a predator's nose, mouth, or eyes.

Some animals are very well protected from their predators, and when they reach adulthood they have practically no enemies.

1. The rhinoceros has three weapons for protection: its large size, its thick skin (almost armored), and its fearful horn. Nobody dares to attack it!

2. A charging elephant is a threatening spectacle for any of its enemies. Many lions have died from being impaled by the tusks or trampled under the feet of an attacking elephant.

3. The painful quills of the African porcupine can grow to 20 inches long and sting a predator for days. As a result, sometimes the wounds become infected and the attacker dies!

The hippopotamus' knife-shaped canines can grow to be almost 2 feet long. With these weapons, it can even split a crocodile in two!

2

Predators have the most powerful weapons

Predators are animals that obtain their food by killing other animals. All predators must be expert hunters, because if they are unable to catch their prey they will die.

There are some predators, such as cats and eagles, that only eat a very specific type of prey. They are called "specialists" and normally live close to their prey. They do not hunt every day because a good kill will provide them with enough food for several days. Other animals kill and devour anything they come across. These animals are called "opportunists," and their lives are much less restful. They travel great distances in search of food.

In order to be successful hunters, predators must be faster, stronger, and smarter than their victims. They also have a group of fearful weapons, such as sharp claws, very powerful venom, sharp beaks, and cutting teeth.

2

1

4

Sharks are the most powerful predators in the ocean. Their many teeth are sharpened like a saw and placed in several rows. When the front teeth fall out, the ones in the next row replace them.

Birds of prey, such as this eagle, have very sharp beaks and powerful claws.

Animals that must hunt for their food have developed fearful "weapons," such as claws, venom, sharp teeth, beaks, etc.

1. The venom of a poisonous snake can end its prey's life in a few seconds.

2. Felines have two weapons: claws and very sharp canine teeth. When they attack, they bite their prey on the neck and kill them through suffocation. When most felines walk, their claws retract so they will not be worn down.

3. The scorpion uses its powerful sting for defense as well as to kill its prey.

4. Crocodiles catch their victims in jaws that close like mousetraps. They submerge their prey in the water and drown them.

3

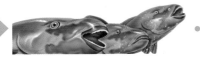
Despite all of that, finding food is hard for everyone

Archerfish watch their prey from beneath the water's surface. Then, they knock the insect into the water and devour it.

Apart from hunting, there are many ways of finding food. An animal's diet often influences its behavior. For example, animals that eat grass—a food with a low energy content—spend much of their time grazing.

An animal's size often has no relation to the kind of food it eats. For example, whales, the biggest animals on the planet, eat krill (tiny crustaceans that are among the smallest). Many dissimilar animals seek out the same food sources; bees and hummingbirds, for example, both dine on flowers.

Some animals, such as vultures, are scavengers, which means that they eat the remains of whatever carcasses they may come across. This system has an advantage in that it does not require them to hunt or kill prey. Of course, the food is not so "fresh" as if they had just hunted it and there is always a risk of contracting disease.

2

3

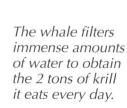

The whale filters immense amounts of water to obtain the 2 tons of krill it eats every day.

All animals, both carnivores and herbivores, struggle to get their food. Because winter forage is particularly hard to find, some animals have learned to gather food in the summer in order to store it in preparation for the lean months of winter.

1. The field mouse accumulates nuts and acorns in its burrow during the fall to see itself through the winter.

2. The hummingbird has developed a very special way of flying and a special beak to access its particular food found in flowers.

3. Chameleons have three "weapons" that they use to surprise their victims. They move slowly, the color of their skin changes to blend into the environment, and they lash out their tongues at great speed to catch insects that are their prey.

4. Some animals, such as these lycaons (African hunting dogs), form groups to hunt, which allows them to catch bigger prey.

4

1

Animals also fight against their own species for their territory and females

In a fight between wolves, the defeated wolf adopts an unmistakable subordinate position that means, "You are in charge here. Please do not hurt me."

One of the main goals in an animal's life is to produce the largest number of offspring possible. Often, males fight among themselves to mate with as many females as they can. The male that leaves the most descendants is the most successful!

However, during these fights, one or both of the combatants may be seriously wounded. So, many species have developed other less "dangerous" systems, which allow the males to measure their strength against one another. Males may show off by pushing one another, locking horns, etc.

Some species, however, do fight for their mates. Lions, for example, have such dreadful fights that frequently the defeated male ends up seriously wounded or even dead!

3

Fights among members of the same species are often ritualistic. The rituals are intended to show off strength while avoiding serious injury to the participants. If there is a big difference in strength between the two fighters, the weakest will usually give up without a fight. When the combatants are about equally matched, the battle can go on for hours.

1. In fights among oryx, the animals' sharp horns can seriously injure an opponent. After all, even lions have died after being stabbed with these weapons.

2. Male giraffes fight by pushing each other with their long necks.

3. Male monitor lizards use their claws to try to knock an opponent down. The winner takes the female.

These beetles have well-developed jaws shaped like "horns" that they use in the fight for territory. Sometimes one of the two rivals dies!

The fight for the female is not always violent

Some species attract mates by means other than fighting. The harmonious songs and glorious multicolored feathers of some male birds make them irresistible to the female of their species. To make their charm even more noticeable, the males may perform dances in order to show their colorful feathers, or even take "gifts" to the females so to convince them of their "good intentions." These gifts may be little branches for the nest, colorful objects, or food.

In many frogs, the males croak powerfully to attract faraway females.

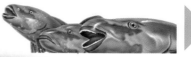

Male tritons (submarine snails) develop combinations of bright colors to attract females during the reproductive season.

Male birds are true experts in mating rituals. Their songs, bright colors, dances, etc., are a spectacle that females cannot resist.

1. The exhibition performed by a male sentinel bird combines complicated movements reminiscent of flamenco dancers.

2. The female peacock has very discreet coloring so as not to attract the attention of predators. On the other hand, the gorgeously plumed males compete among themselves with more spectacular colors.

3. Male prairie roosters always look for the best place to show off their bright colors.

1

2

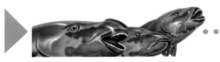

Glossary

Carnivores: Meat eaters.

Feline: Animals that belong to the cat family, such as tigers, lions, etc.

Harem: Group of female animals that reproduce only with one specific male.

Hierarchy: Degrees of power upon which the members of a group are organized. The dominant animal is the strongest and most privileged.

Krill: Little crustaceans that are the main element in the diet of whales.

Migrations: Major journeys made by animals searching for areas with better pastures or more adequate opportunities for reproducing.

Predators: Animals that must watch and attack other animals to get their food.

Prey: Animals that are captured and eaten by others.

Scavengers: Animals that eat the remains of dead creatures. Many times the meat is already rotten.

Index